Dental Websi

DEMYSTIFIED

Dental Websites
DEMYSTIFIED

Taking the Mystery
Out of Finding Patients Online

David J. Larson

Dedication

This book is dedicated to all the dental professionals. Thank you for your gifts of health and playing such a vital role in ending pain and suffering in this world.

Acknowledgments

Being a CEO of a company and trying to write a book is ambitious. Some say crazy. I could not have done this without someone close to me to keep things running smoothly both at home and the office. That person for me is Tina Larson, my wife of 27 years (and counting). Thank you for your support and encouragement through this whole process. Thank you for helping to keep the plates spinning. As far as I know, none hit the floor.

To my sons, Daniel and Brian, thank you for allowing me so much time to devote to this project. I know it was "different" having your father at home during the day. I appreciate the food runs and support. It was great to be with you.

To the amazing people at Sales & Marketing Technologies, you know this wouldn't have happened without all the knowledge you've shared. There are so many people who have helped me over the years I couldn't possibly name them all. To the literally hundreds (maybe thousands) of people who have shared their technical knowledge, expertise and insights with me over the years, I am forever grateful. I have to mention just a few—David Ajoy, Bernie Piekarski, Jimmy Smith, Ken Anthony, Alison Clement, Russell Troutman, Todd Mittleman, Terry Howard, Robert Marsa, Chuck Southworth, Debbie Morris, Joe Methven, and Chris Mitchell. Thank you all for your wisdom.

I would like to mention a few who had tremendous impact at critical points in my life. Without them my life wouldn't have taken this path. First, my father, John E. Larson, who bought my first IBM PC in 1982.

Little did I know what amazing things would come out of that box. To Wil Dershimer, Jr., my computer science teacher at Seminole Community College, who gave me the solid knowledge base and training to get started in computers. To Donald Fuller, my first marketing professor at UCF, who got me interested in the marketing industry. To Ray Fisk, marketing professor and friend, who with one sentence changed my life forever—"Dave, you should get involved with the Internet. It is going to change the world." That was not an understatement! I am so glad I took Ray's advice.

To Michelle Prince and Cheryl Callighan-Barrett at Prince Performance Publishing, thank you for helping me get my book out. I would have never attempted this without your wisdom and belief in me. Thank you to Leah Humphries at Five Star Branding for the cover design.

A special thank you to Howard Berg and Diane Lampe for helping birth the idea for this book. Last but not least, thanks to Lon Winter for his encouragement and assistance in the writing process. Thank you all for your wise counsel.

Table of Contents

How This Book Will Benefit You

THIS BOOK IS designed to help dentists and their office managers build websites capable of attracting patients to your practice. This book is the collective wisdom of more than 22 years in the marketing business. This book will help you make the most of your #1 marketing asset—your website.

Whether you have a website now or are planning a new one, this book can help you improve what you have and make sure you are positioned to be successful at marketing your practice in the future.

I wrote this from an owner/manager perspective so you are aware of your website options, know what you are buying, and who you are buying from. I want you to understand how to manage the website building and marketing process.

What this book is not. I know there are already a lot of books on Web Development out there. The vast majority are written from a technical development standpoint. This book is not designed to teach you how to build your own website. Quite frankly, I don't believe that you, a highly skilled dental professional, should ever be developing your own website. I don't care what they say on TV. Your time is too valuable. Building and marketing your website should be left to a highly skilled website development professional.

This book will help you make wise choices about what you need and what you don't need. So before someone talks you into spending several hours a day on social media, you'll already know that is likely to be a poor investment of your time.

What I want you to get out of this book is an understanding about what makes up a great website. By understanding the critical elements of a great website, you will be able to make good decisions when it comes to creating your own website.

I will do my best to explain everything simply and in a manner that will enable you to go out, deal in your marketplace and get the right website for you and your practice. I know this information will be helpful, so let's get started.

Deciding Who Should
Handle Your Website

YOUR WEBSITE IS (and will remain) the critical cornerstone when it comes to marketing your practice. Websites have become much more complex than the small static websites of old. They are interactive now, they do things, they involve programming and coordination with other outside programs. The marketing environment in which they exist is also more complex. The search engines your website is trying to impress are much more sophisticated—they watch every move, load time, duplicate content, bogus links, number and order of words. They exist in an increasingly social world with immediate feedback. The people who use them have changed too. They are more mobile and more knowledgeable about the Internet.

So, before you start looking for a website solution, you need to think about who will be in charge of running your new practice website. You may think you have that handled—your staff will do it. That is fine. However, you need to know whether they have the skills needed to manage today's practice website.

To determine whether they have the skills, you need to look at these four areas: technical expertise, marketing expertise, writing skills and available time. A deficit in any of these areas can be a serious reason to reconsider any plans you might have to use internal staff to help with the creation and maintenance of your website.

First question: How technical is my staff?

Some websites can be very technical. If your people are not good at using computers and software, then you may want to look for a simpler solution. If you want a powerful, full-featured, state-of-the-art website and your staff is not technical, you may be better off not having them handle the website at all. I tell our clients:

- The more powerful the software, generally the more features you have.

- The more features you have, generally the more complex the software.

- The more complex the software, generally the more technical expertise is required.

Second question: Do any of my staff have a marketing, advertising, communications, or sales background?

Websites are all about fresh, updated content. The message and how it is communicated is important. If you happen to have someone who can answer "yes" to this question, you are fortunate. Having someone on staff with a marketing background will prove to be helpful when managing the content on your website. If the answer is "no" to this question, then strongly consider getting outside help with content and maintenance of the site.

Third question: Does the person I am considering tasking with website maintenance have good writing skills?

Writing skill is a deal killer. The Internet shows how your practice looks to the world. If you have grammar and spelling mistakes on your website they can negatively impact the impression of your practice. If the writing skills aren't up to par, don't use them.

Fourth question: How much available time does your staff have to maintain a website?

Depending on the size, complexity, and effort being put into your website, maintenance of the site can run anywhere from a few hours a month for small, static websites to full-time dedicated staff members for those engaged in large-scale blogging and social media. However, for most dental offices, a few hours a week should be sufficient. If your staff has the extra time (and they write well), consider using them for routine edits. If not, you can outsource 100% if need be.

One last thing I would caution you about is having one person who knows and runs everything. If you lose that person, it puts you in a precarious position. I call it "having to change a flat while running 55 miles an hour." That means if you lose that person, you need to find someone immediately who can come up to speed without missing a beat. It leads to high pressure hiring, which we all know is not good.

We favor a team approach when running a website. We like multiple eyes watching out for problems. We like having several people cross-trained. That way, they can take over in a pinch if someone leaves.

There are a few more possibilities . . .

Fifth question: Should I (the dentist) do the website?

Some of my more technical dentist friends are sitting there thinking, "I could do it! I could knock out a website in a week!" Maybe you could. However, is it wise? Getting the website up is one thing. If you're running a practice or managing a practice do you really have time to stay on top of Internet marketing and web changes along with everything else you do?

I would say "No!" We are looking for a long-term solution. Over the long haul, both the Internet and dentistry will continue to grow and evolve quickly. Faster and faster, new innovations will appear. Social media just came on a few years back and it completely changed the way Internet marketing works today. You may already be feeling this accelerating rate of change.

If you don't have the skills, the time, or the drive, it's an easy decision to hire a company to build your website. What if you have a new practice and are short of money? Those enticing ads say that you can do it yourself for $3.95 a month. *Don't do it!* Even though there are do-it-yourself tools and they give you all these promises, it isn't easy and it is time consuming. To be honest, I have tried a lot of these "easy do-it-yourself tools," and most are pretty terrible at both design and marketing. Don't waste your valuable time. You are much better off getting a real website for your practice than using these tools.

Question 6: I have an IT person. Can I have them build our website?

You can do whatever you want. However, let me give you one more piece of advice. Let IT people handle the computers, and let the marketers handle your website. Even if you have a knowledgeable IT person, I don't recommend letting them build your website. Why? Because you need a marketing professional to market your practice.

We have IT people. I love them and I work with them every day. But most of them are not marketers. While technically they can build you a website, it will probably not be very appealing to your potential patients. Appealing to potential patients is what we are trying to achieve. I am sorry if I've offended any IT friends. They are good people. They want to help. However, their talents are better served in other areas like running servers and hosting—not design. That's all.

Now that you have an idea of who might be able to help you, and who should not help you, let's talk about what you want your website to do.

Setting the Objectives
of Your Website

AMONG THE FIRST things I like to find out from our clients are their objectives. What do they want to accomplish? If they have an existing website, what do they like, or why are they looking to change? To get your imagination cooking, here are some of the most often stated dental website objectives.

Get new patients. People are people so there will always be patient turnover. Getting new patients should always be on top of the list. If your website is done properly, it should be producing a steady flow of new patients. If not, you need to keep working on it until it does.

Brand the practice. Your website is your primary marketing vehicle for promoting your practice. It should be mentioned in every form of marketing that you do. That way, when prospective patients go to check you out (and they will) you have a quality source of information representing your practice.

Separate your practice from the competition. You want a website that tells your story. A powerful story builds value in the mind of the prospective patients. Done right, this presentation of your practice will separate you from other practices. It will let the patient know what makes you unique.

Make things easier on the patients. Streamline the process for first-time patients by having the forms on the website. This can cut down or eliminate the time it takes for a new patient to become part of your practice. New patients can be nervous on their first visit. Having their paperwork prepared before they come in can ease their stress levels. The new patient will feel prepared and under control and have a more pleasant first experience.

Provide patient education. There are many sources of medical information online. That being said, you may wish to include some information about your procedures on your website. It can be a two-edged sword, however. Depending on the quality of the content, the "education" can be either helpful or harmful. Helpful, it is additional content for your website and can prepare a patient for what to expect. Harmful, is if things sound too scary or you show graphic pictures it can cause patients to reconsider treatment.

Get feedback from your patients. It can be wise to survey patients after you've cared for them, just to be sure they are happy. It helps you spot problems early. Not everyone fills out the survey. However, better to ask and be ignored than not ask and learn too late that there is a problem.

Reduce patient reminders. Sending electronic voice, text and e-mail patient reminders can reduce manual follow up. These electronic reminders can lower the cost of missed appointments and help improve timely arrival.

Cut time spent scheduling appointments. Depending on the practice, it might be a good thing to have your patients manage and change their own appointments. They can do this online and in some cases reduce missed appointments.

Cut routine support calls. Your website can answer routine questions by including something as simple as a detailed "About Us" section. It can also eliminate calls such as "can you give me directions?" or "can you give me your address?" or "what hours are you open?"

Increase the value of your practice before selling. A website producing new patient leads can increase the value of your practice. So even if you're thinking it's near the finish line for me, don't neglect it. It's never too late to do a website.

Build a greater connection with your patients. A well-designed website can help people learn more about you. Staying in touch with your patients via electronic newsletters and social media can also help people become more familiar with you. The closer you are to your patients, the more likely they are to refer new patients to you.

Once you know what you want to accomplish (your objectives), then it is time to start pulling your act together. The more of this information you have ready, the less your website will ultimately cost.

What You'll Need to Build Your Website

ASSUMING SOMEONE IS building your website for you, there are really just three things you need to get it done right:

1. COMPUTER WITH INTERNET CONNECTION

This, of course, should go without saying. Even if someone else will be building your website, you still need a computer (an iPad or tablet is not recommended). During the building process, you need to be able to send information to your website developer in digital form. Also, when you launch your website you will need to communicate electronically with people contacting you through the website. You can't do that effectively without a computer.

2. KNOWLEDGE OF YOUR MARKET

It is important to get an idea of the type of people for whom you are building the website. Try to gain an understanding of who lives in the area immediately around your practice. If you have demographic information on your patients, that is a great place to start. Pull a sample of some patient records. How old are they? Who is the main person who contacts you? Are they male or female? Did they come in as a family? If so, what age are the children? How did they find you? How long have they been with you? How much do they typically spend in a year? If it is a new practice, have a research company pull some demographics on your area. All this information is valuable to know.

Finally, take some time to search for your type of business online. Go to Google and Bing and search your area to see who your competitors are. Visit and go through their websites. This way you can get the lay of the land. Save this research and share it with your web developer when the time comes. It is important that both of you know about your market.

3. WEBSITE CONTENT

Website content is what you have on the website—your copy, your pictures, your audio, your videos and pretty much anything else that's not the programming structure of the website.

Since website content is what you need to provide to the developer, let's go over each part so you know how to pull it together.

Gathering Your Website Content

CONTENT IS ALL the information that goes into a website. Pull together all written information, logos, pictures, videos, testimonials, etc., in electronic form. Include past websites, brochures, ads, news stories, and awards. The more content the web developer has, the better the site will likely be.

Put it on a USB drive so it is portable. Organize into folders like: Photos, Logos, Website Copy, Video. This will help the designers know what it is and where it will be used. Having it organized will save you money in the development process. Make sure all photos are high resolution.

WHY WEBSITE CONTENT IS IMPORTANT

Website content is getting to be one of the most critical pieces of a website. It's important because this is what the search engines are looking at to help determine what is on your site and the rankings. It's important because it's what the visitors are viewing to determine whether or not to use your services.

From the search engine's perspective, they realize that users get very unhappy if they go to a website that isn't relevant to what they are searching for. So Google, Bing, Yahoo and the others work very hard to make sure the websites they are sending you to are relevant to your search. Because relevance is so critical, Google, for one, has given it very heavy weighting in the rankings of your website. It is so important, Google won't even rank you in the paid searches if it isn't "in their opinion" relevant.

The good news is that the search engines are getting a lot better at reading what is on your website. The bad news is you still can't trust that they can read everything that is on it. You still need an SEO expert to help the search engine spiders see everything and understand what is on the pages.

Content that moves people to action

Keep the search engines happy and you will have traffic to your website. However, traffic alone isn't enough. You have to make it interesting to the visitor and not be like reading like a textbook. Tons of websites have traffic, but do the visitors contact the practice and book appointments? You need to make sure you have quality content that will motivate people to take action. The goal is to get people to know, like and trust you. Straight text and a few pictures of teeth isn't enough. We talked about it before. Do you have some videos on the website? Videos help to get a visual image of you and your practice. You are inviting them to become involved with your practice or stay involved with your practice.

One critical element you need to include in your website content is a Call To Action (CTA). A call to action asks the visitor to take some specific action toward becoming a patient. You may want to consider including multiple calls to action on your website to appeal to different types of buyers. Here are some examples of calls to actions: Fill out the contact form, book an appointment, ask to receive a first-timer discount on x-rays, subscribe (opt-in) to receive a newsletter, or download a free report. What you offer is only limited by your imagination. You want to make the offer appealing to the prospective patient so that they will share their information with you. If the prospective patient doesn't take action or share their contact info with you, your staff won't have any way to follow up with them. Calls to action are extremely important. The right CTA can seriously improve the ROI of your website.

THE WEBSITE COPY

The three basic content writing options:

you can write the website copy;

you can hire someone to write the website copy; or

you can use off-the-shelf copy.

If you write the copy . . .

This can be the least expensive way or the most expensive way, depending on how you value your time.

Pros: You know your practice better than anyone, it comes from your heart, nothing is lost in translation, and it may clarify some things as you write it.

Cons: You are probably not trained on how to write copy, you may not be a good writer, it may come out too clinical, and it may take a while.

If you hire someone to write the copy . . .

It may cost a few shekels to do this, but the end result is usually better.

Pros: Better quality work, usually faster, easier, more appealing to the reader, doesn't take up much of your time and a copywriter will come up with angles and ideas you would never come up with on your own.

Cons: Cost

I recommend most people hire a professional copywriter to write your copy. If you do hire a copywriter, be sure to participate in the process. I say this because you know things about your practice that nobody else knows. If you go the route of the professional copywriter, here is what you can expect. Typically, the copywriter will do some research, then call and interview you. They will write the first draft of your copy. They will send you the first draft for changes and suggestions. You comment, edit and/or make any changes and send that back to the copywriter. The copywriter goes through it again making revisions and then they deliver the final version of the copy to you. The revision part may repeat one more time if needed.

Using Off-The-Shelf Copy . . .

Some providers give you websites with website copy that is pre-loaded in the website they deliver to you. In some cases, they claim that the copy is pre-optimized for the search engines. These developers tend to use the same copy for all their dental websites.

Pros: You have something to start with, it is free, and it may be optimized.

Cons: Search engines will penalize you for using it verbatim. You may not own the rights to take the copy with you if you move the website. Prospects may see it elsewhere. It won't capture your unique identity if you use it as is.

The thinking behind this off-the-shelf copy is two-fold:

1) It makes it easier to write your own copy if you are not starting with a blank white page; and

2) If they can figure out what works in the search engines once, all their clients from then on can benefit.

This tactic worked fine for a while, however, people started abusing it. They found what worked well and built, in some cases, hundreds of sites to dominate a category. Some websites were grabbing content off other sites (called scraping) and Google was forced to crack down.

Google now has an algorithm that will analyze your site for unique copy. Google can actually tell if your website was the very first website with your copy. If it wasn't the first to have it, Google's algorithm puts a big hit on your page rank so your site falls in the rankings.

Advice if your website comes with off-the-shelf copy—Do not launch your site with off-the-shelf copy. If your developer includes starter copy, use it as a guide, but be sure to rewrite it. You don't have to change every word. However, it's best to make a substantial (90%) change. Do not use copy spinner software either. Google is on to that as well.

Some people may consider it okay to "borrow" copy from somebody else. It is not legal to take someone else's copy. You don't want to do that. Nothing would be more embarrassing and threatening to your good name and reputation than to get nailed for copyright violation.

How to see if someone has stolen your copy . . .

To catch online copy thieves, I simply embed some unique copy phrases in our website copy. Every six months or so, I do a search for this unique copy. My record is having caught 20 websites using my stolen copy. What you do from there to the infringers is up to you.

One final piece of advice on all copy - Keep in mind, you're writing for patients not doctors. If you undertake the copywriting process yourself, have someone else review it. You may be using technical terms without even realizing it. You need to think like a patient. You need to see the world as your patients view the world. The whole goal is to make sure your website copy appeals to them.

Copy is a very important part of your website content. It needs to appeal to both reader and search engine. Get some help on it.

LOGO ART

Does your practice have a logo? If so, you want to get it in electronic form so you can e-mail it to your website developer. If you don't have a logo, you should have one professionally produced. It will greatly add to the professional image of your practice. Prices for logos have really come down. They used to be thousands of dollars for a good one. Now, you can get one starting at about $500.

PHOTOS

Pull together all the pictures of your practice. If you don't have some recent photos, hire a professional photographer in your area to come and take some. Do not scrimp when it comes to your photos. High quality photos are the easiest way to enhance your image on the web. They make a huge difference. The more photos you have of your actual practice the more custom your website will be.

When researching photographers, always look at their portfolio. Many photographers have specialties—like some are good at portrait photography, some are good at shooting food pictures, some are good at sports where there is movement, some are good at shooting offices (they call that environmental photography). You are looking for someone who is good at environmental and portrait photography. The portfolio will give you signs that you've found the right photographer.

While the photographer is there, have them take head shots of everyone in the office. If you like, you can post their picture with their bio. It really looks professional when they all are consistent. It is also a nice touch to give a copy to your employees on disk so they have a nice photo of themselves. I did this, and many of our employees told me this was the first time they had a professional picture taken since high school. I think they really liked them because I see many of them still use the images on Facebook.

Other ideas. When you take your pictures, make sure you have people in them. An empty office looks cold.

It can be very powerful to have Before and After shots. Make sure it is your work and isn't stock photography.

If I were you, I would pass on photos depicting what happens during a procedure. That freaks patients out. You don't want to scare off pa-tients. The same is true with showing scary looking dental instruments. Don't show these on your website.

VIDEO

Video can be very effective too because it allows you to give a person-alized message to the viewers of your website. Video is really optional; however, it can be very effective. Some would say it's not optional. If you are going to do video, again, pay a professional to do it. You can't believe the quality difference. It is like YouTube vs. Network television. No comparison.

VIDEO PRODUCTION

If you plan to be in the video, then you need to work with a local company that will either come out or shoot the video on-site or have you come to their studio.

If you would prefer not to be in the video and have a professional actor handle the speaking parts, you can source that locally or outside your area. If you don't know who to call, my company Sales & Market-ing Technologies can help arrange some reasonably priced, high quality video services for you. All you have to do is call our office at 1-800-434-0339 and tell them you would like some help arranging a videographer.

TESTIMONIALS

Testimonials are easy to get. Just ask a few clients who are happy with your work if they could fill out either a comment card or send you a letter. Be sure to get their permission to use it on your website.

If you are using social media, you can get testimonials the easy way by asking people if they will give you a recommendation. Some of the online systems that do reviews of your practice also make it easy for patients to leave testimonials.

Now that you have done your research, you know your objectives, and you have your content ready, it is almost time to pick a web development company to work with. However, before you run loose and start talking to potential developers, I want you to know a bit more about the tools developers use so you can make an informed decision on which developer's solution might be best for you.

Tools for Managing Websites: Content Management Systems

THE FIRST THING I want you to know is you have the option of getting your website built with or without a Content Management System (CMS). A content management system allows you (or someone on your staff) to go in and make changes to your website. Usually, you can change text and graphics using the CMS. If you see a little typo or a word that needs to be changed, you can go in and fix it and it won't cost you anything for the change. Even though most CMS software lets you change the graphics, I recommend you leave the graphic work to the professionals. That is more involved. You might wind up breaking something on the page.

If you would like to make changes yourself and you have someone fairly technical to make them, then you may want a Content Management System. If you know you will never touch the site, you don't necessarily need a CMS. Given the choice, I personally would want one. I like the ability to make changes on my own without learning how to program. For our discussion, let's assume you will most likely get a CMS.

Some people never plan on touching the site and don't care about what tools the developers use. If you are among those who don't care, that is fine. I recommend at least asking the developer what they are going to use to build your website, and then read the section that applies to what you are buying. The tools they use have a long-term impact on your cost of ownership. Probably a better idea is to read it before you buy. That way you know what you are signing up for.

TWO MAJOR QUESTIONS: STANDARD OR CUSTOM, OPEN OR CLOSED

If you can answer these two major questions you can save yourself a ton of time talking to the wrong web development companies.

Standard or Custom?

The first question you have to answer is, do you want a standard (template) type website or do you want a custom website? Translation—are you on a budget (look for a standard dental website) or are you open to upgrading your website to something that really makes your practice stand out (look for custom)?

Standard websites

Standard websites are built by companies that generally mass-produce sites. You have probably seen where several dentists have the same looking site. Some have almost exactly the same content except for their bio, address and phone number. They either have a standard design they copy to make the website, or they have website building software that you set up using a template design.

The standard websites are much less expensive and are usually much less flexible than custom websites. You basically get what you get. You can't really change them all that much.

Custom websites

Custom websites means the website is built specifically for you. Usually, there is a huge difference between customized and custom websites. All developers will tell you they customize your website; however, the true custom web developer can write custom code and can create custom features on your website that are unique to you. The process is different. The custom developer consults with you and then builds a website to your exact needs, requirements and desires.

Custom websites cost more because there are extra steps in development; however, you get exactly the look and functionality you want. The website, when finished, is one of a kind.

Source: Open or Closed?

The website you buy from a web developer will either be Closed Source, or Open Source. The open or closed discussion will get into the nuts and bolts a bit. This is a very important question. The outcome of this one question will determine the programming language and database your website will be built on. If you find the discussion contains more detail than you want to know, at least skim the advantages and disadvantages.

Closed source websites do not give you access to the programming source code of the website. You can't see the programming language it was written in. You can make changes to the website, you just can't modify the underlying programming code yourself without help from the developer.

Open source websites come with full access to the underlying programming source code. You can see the programming language it was written in. You can modify the underlying programming code yourself. Whether that is wise to do is another issue.

Since there are many types of open and closed source software, for our discussion we'll be talking about open and closed source Web Application Frameworks and Content Management Systems. Simply put, this is the software written to create and manage websites.

A couple of things you should know...

Most web developers have very strong opinions about open source tools vs. closed source, usually to the point of being zealots. If you bring it up, the method they use is the best way. They will pooh-pooh the other method of development. Listening to them, you would think you would die if you use the other type of software to develop your website. Don't be thrown off by this. Both open source and closed source have advantages and disadvantages.

Since my company offers both closed source and open source solutions, I will do my best to tell you balanced pros and cons of each. I am 100% certain that not everyone will agree with my opinions. I am giving you a broad view. If you look hard enough, everything I am about to tell you has exceptions. Let's take the easier one first.

CLOSED SOURCE (PROPRIETARY) WEBSITES

What Is It?

Closed Source website software is software created to run a website. The creator (developer) of the software is called the licensor. You, as a user, are the licensee. You, as the licensee, can run the software; however, you cannot access the programming source code. You, as the licensee, cannot modify the source code yourself. The software still works. However, you just can't get all the way down to the programming source code.

If you need modifications, you can always contact the developer (or someone authorized) to make them for you. Do you have to modify the software? No. It should be fully functioning without modification.

For both the Closed and Open Source discussion it is important to understand the concept of access to code. So let's give an example you should be able to relate to. Something you probably already own—Microsoft Word.

If you are using Microsoft Word, are you aware that it is Closed Source software? It is! You don't own nor can you access the programming source code to Microsoft Word. Microsoft owns it and they don't give access to it. So how does this arrangement work? When you purchased the software, you received a license from Microsoft to use the software.

You have the right to use the software. You can install it. It works. You can even go into the Word program and make any changes (move buttons around, etc.) that Microsoft allows you to make. You can customize the product to your needs. However, you can't get down to the actual programming source code Microsoft wrote it in and make changes there. Should this trouble you that you don't have access? For hundreds of millions of users, the answer is "No." They aren't programmers. They wouldn't know what to do if they were given access. They could care less. They just want it to work.

It is pretty much the same with Closed Source website software. For most normal users, they just want it to work. It does.

Advantages of Websites Created Using Closed Source (Proprietary) Tools:

- **One company to deal with for support** – If you have any problems, you call the closed source developer and they take care of it.

- **Bugs are not your problem** – The closed source developer will fix any bugs.

- **Developer will customize** – If the developer offers to customize, you contact them and they will make the changes. You have to go through them because they have access to the code.

- **Less security risk** – Since the developer created the code they know what's in it and what's not. Generally, there is less chance for security problems because fewer people have knowledge of the internal workings of the program.

- **Tighter integration** – Generally the software works easier because the developer took the time to plan out what is going into the product.

- **Easier to use and manage** – Updates are generally easier and less frequent because the developers generally don't have to plan for thousands of contingencies from hundreds of developers and their add-ons.

Disadvantages of Websites Created Using Closed Source (Proprietary) Tools:

- **Vendor lock-in** – You can be dependent on one vendor for changes. This isn't always true, but assume it is true for your website. If the vendor is good, it can actually be a good thing. A bad vendor can be a bad thing.

- **Paid upgrades** – Because you are dealing with professionals who are being paid to improve their product, their cost has to be covered if you want improvements.

- **Smaller choice of available options** – A closed source developer has to pay upfront for options to be developed, so there are usually fewer options. These options are generally market-based, meaning they have been most requested. Open source by comparison, may have thousands of options. In some cases, even tens of thousands of options.

Closed Source Advice:

- **Check out the developer and make sure they have been around a while** – If they haven't, ask what will happen in the event they go out of business? What is their code written in? Will you get access to the code in the event they go out of business?

- **Let the company you buy from host** – If you pick a proprietary solution have them do everything. That way, you know who to talk to if something doesn't work right.

- **Find out if you can move your website to another host** – Hopefully, you will be happy and you won't need to move it. However, you don't want to find out later you purchased from a vendor you can't live with and you can't move the site.

- **Get clarity on your needs upfront** – In the planning process, make sure that the software has most of the features you need. If it doesn't, ask the developer for an estimate to add the features you want. If it is too much, try to find another solution that is a little closer to your needs.

- **Budget for upgrades** – It is wise to keep your website up-to-date and using current technology. So you'll need to budget for upgrades, however your developer charges for them. Some of them have annual maintenance fees; some of them just have you pay as you upgrade. Most are reasonable. So just make sure you're planning for that and then any features that you need as well.

- **See samples of their work** – It is always good to see some sample sites. Try out some of the features you would like to get. That way you can see how well they work.

- **Set deadlines** – It costs more to have development projects drag on. Set deadlines for your developer and then make sure you both stick with them.

- **Make sure you like the development support staff** – Chances are you will be working with them for a while. It helps if you like the team you'll be working with.

OPEN SOURCE WEBSITES

What Is It?

Open Source website software is software created to run a website. The base programming source code (software) is made available for free distribution under a Public License. You (the licensee) have access to and can make changes to the underlying source code. The base code is made available usually at no charge in hopes that others will create enhancements to it.

How does Open Source work? Typically, a group of programmers with a similar interest will come together to get an open source project started. They will create a large block of code called the "core" as the basis for the project. Then other programmers seeing the core will come behind them to develop add-on enhancements called plug-ins or modules for the core. These plug-ins may or may not be free.

When someone says your website will be open source they are saying your website will be built using the open source software code. To most people, open source just means free software and you can get to the source code and change it. If only it were that simple.

Free comes with strings attached. Like closed source, there are license agreements with terms you must abide by. Most open source software uses public licenses that can be very complex. To see a few of the major ones, go to: http://en.wikipedia.org/wiki/Comparison_of_free_ and_open-source_software_licenses

According to Wikipedia, the most widely used one is the GNU public license. To get a flavor for what it contains, go to: http://en.wikipedia. org/wiki/GNU_General_Public_License

I am not an attorney. Though I have been involved with reading and writing many legal agreements, I read some of these license agreements and I can barely follow the fine points of what they are saying. They map out things like how the software is distributed, the source code, the derived works, the integrity of the author's source code, you must not discriminate against persons or groups or discriminate against fields or endeavors. You've got to be able to have the license be redistributed without the need of execution of additional license by those parties. What is acceptable linking and unacceptable linking?...blah, blah, blah.

The whole intent is to provide free distribution of software programming code. You're supposed to give back to the community for helping you. In other words, you've got a community of programmers providing this work for free. If you or your programmer improve or enhance something, you're supposed to give it back to the community. Sounds very noble. But in a litigious world where big money is made (or lost) on

Intellectual Property, suddenly something very simple got very complex.

I don't know why all open source licenses can't be like the amazingly easy to understand jQuery MIT License. It is just a few lines long. So few, I'll print it here . . .

Copyright 2012 jQuery Foundation and other contributors http://jquery.com/

Permission is hereby granted, free of charge, to any person obtaining a copy of this software and associated documentation files (the "Software"), to deal in the Software without restriction, including without limitation the rights to use, copy, modify, merge, publish, distribute, sub license, and/or sell copies of the Software, and to permit persons to whom the Software is furnished to do so, subject to the following conditions:

The above copyright notice and this permission notice shall be included in all copies or substantial portions of the Software.

THE SOFTWARE IS PROVIDED "AS IS", WITHOUT WARRANTY OF ANY KIND, EXPRESS OR IMPLIED, INCLUDING BUT NOT LIMITED TO THE WARRANTIES OF MERCHANTABILITY, FITNESS FOR A PARTICULAR PURPOSE AND NON INFRINGEMENT. IN NO EVENT SHALL THE AUTHORS OR COPYRIGHT HOLDERS BE LIABLE FOR ANY CLAIM, DAMAGES OR OTHER LIABILITY, WHETHER IN AN ACTION OF CONTRACT, TORT OR OTHERWISE, ARISING FROM, OUT OF OR IN CONNECTION WITH THE SOFTWARE OR THE USE OR OTHER DEALINGS IN THE SOFTWARE.

I am pretty sure most people can understand what this says. I think if all open source licenses were this clear it would be better for the industry as a whole.

I can't comment on the risks of using open source. I will say I have only seen a handful of cases where they went after a big company that they felt wasn't abiding by the terms of the license.

Would "they" come after a dentist for a violation of some obscure condition in the GNU license? I don't know. I have never heard of any such case. All I know is that many millions of websites are built using open source. So I must assume, as long as you are not a billion dollar corporation, it is an acceptable risk.

Examples of open source software

Here are a few of the major open source ones: WordPress, Drupal, Joomla, and DotNetNuke. Most open source programs are written in PHP (an open source programming language). However, there are open source programs written in other languages. DotNetNuke, for example, is written in Microsoft's .Net.

Open source advantages:

- **Low price** – The core software is free. If your needs are modest and you can find a close match for what you need, you will find savings. Provided everything works right, it can be a lower cost option.

- **Speed of development** – A few developers once told me that they could have a site up in fifteen minutes. That's assuming it is a simple site you are building. Obviously, that does not include loading your content. I put them to the test and I saw a 3.5 hour WordPress website. So far, I haven't seen a 15-minute site. So we better just say, if your developer knows their way around the plug-ins, they can assemble your site very quickly.

- **Lots of plug-ins** – I was looking around and the last time I looked at WordPress there were close to twenty-five thousand plug-ins. So that's literally drinking out of the fire hose as far as plug-ins go.

Open Source Disadvantages:

- **Open Source software is free like a puppy is free** – The initial code is free. Then it must be maintained or it becomes a security risk.

If you maintain it, things change. If things change, it breaks other things. It takes time to make open source software work right and keep it working. So sooner or later the developer will have to extract money from you for maintenance and support. If they don't, it is doubtful that they will stay around or be in business to support you.

- **Security** – The minute you let people see how your code is written, you have a bigger security problem than if you didn't. The open source code is wide open for the entire world to see.

- **Numerous upgrades** – There's a lot changing so there are many upgrades to open source and its plug-ins. The open source part of WordPress said we have updates every day. Let's say you've got twenty plug-ins that you're using and everybody has updates, it is a constant thing. The more plug-ins you have, the more maintenance may be required.

- **Multiple people involved** – There really is not a single company behind the whole thing. It is an unpaid community of developers. They are generally very knowledgeable and in many cases don't have the best bedside manner. They don't need to explain a lot to each other because they're all pretty high level programming folks. They expect you to be fairly technical or they will run out of patience quickly with you.

- **Dirty code** – Most of the programmers writing open source are volunteering their time. Cleaning the code is a dry, monotonous, thankless task. Since the programmers don't get paid to go back and clean it up, generally they don't.

- **Hard to get answers** – When it comes to open source, technically there isn't any support other than community support. Either a cryptic online forum or someone out of the goodness of his or her heart will take the time to help you. If something breaks or doesn't work, it's not like you pick up the phone and call a company like Apple and get support. It's not like that. You are on your own to fix the prob-lem yourself or you have to call (and pay) an open source developer.

Once, on behalf of a client, I called a company that specialized in Drupal hosting. Our client, who was hosting there, got a notice out of the blue to move their website to another server at the host. It was a unique hosting environment. I asked if they could help me with that. They said, "We don't offer support." I asked if they could recommend a consultant who was familiar with them? He said "no" and hung up. Not even a goodbye. It amazed me that they could stay in business treating people like that. The point is, with open source you can find yourself on your own.

- **Hard to tell who is qualified and who is not** – Open source's low price and easy initial setup attracts hordes of low skilled, non-tech-nical developers. I call them Dabblers. These are people who get into the web development business to make a few extra dollars. They read a couple of books. They get some business cards. Hey, they are now a "web developer." One way to spot them is they usually charge very low prices. Have you seen the $299 websites? Maybe they can build a very basic site; however, many times they have no clue about security. They don't really know what they're looking at when it comes to the PHP code. If anything hiccups, and it will, they don't know how to fix it. If your business goes for this, you can quickly find yourself in trouble.

- **Low profit equals companies going belly up** – Turnover among open source companies can be very high. Low prices mean they don't make a lot of money. If they don't make a lot of money then they can't stay in business. And if they can't stay in business they dis-appear. So you may start working with somebody and then they quickly take a job with another company and you're on your own. It can happen with open source plug-ins too. If a developer one day wakes up and says I am not going to do this any more. You can be left without support or upgrades. So be aware of that.

- **Template design** – Boring websites start with boring design. To keep prices down, many open source developers use themes. Themes are free or low cost design templates. Since programmers are not designers, a lot of them use themes. You can find nice ones if you have the time. From what I have seen, the cheap ones are not the greatest design.

- **Complexity from expansion** – The area where you go to update and maintain your content is called the back-end manager. As you add and add plug-ins, a simple open source manager can become a complex beast. The more you add to it, the more that can go wrong and the more time it requires to maintain.

- **Code not complete** – The draw to open source is there is generally no charge for the core software itself. You can take it and use it for your purposes. That being said, a fair amount of what is out there in the way of plug-ins are incomplete applications. That's right. It isn't fully built or is buggy. Your developer will need to do some work on it to make it work. So even if you find stuff that works, at a minimum, you'll have to assemble the parts. So it's kind of like that barbecue grill that you get at Christmas, right, and it has a thousand pieces and says, "some assembly required".

- **Hard to separate the good from the bad** – It has been said, you can't step foot in the same river twice. Open source is a fast moving river. It is always changing. Not all plug-ins are created equal. Like WordPress with its 24,000+ plug-ins, it is a daunting task to figure out what are the good ones and what are the bad ones. Even if you find the one that works, with updates regularly being issued, it may break down the road.

- **No warranty** – So if it was a good plug-in and an update was released that made it stop working, is it a good or bad plug-in? I guess it depends on how long it takes you to fix it. Yes, it is your problem.

Open Source Advice:

- **Look for a company that is really in the business** – Your dental practice website is critical to your business. Don't hire a fly-by-night company or some kid in a basement who will just slap you up a website and then leave you to fend for yourself. Pass if they aren't set up to offer support services. There's no warranty with open source. Get a company that can support your practice. Sooner or later you will need it.

- **Get a real programmer to support open source** – One thing the open source people always tout is "Hey you are not tied to us. If things don't work out, you can take it to someone else and they can work on it." While that may be technically true, no one likes cleaning up someone else's mess. You are playing with fire unless you have a highly technical, knowledgeable, experienced Open Source PHP programmer standing by. There are just too many things that can happen to trust it to a non-programmer.

- **Find a professional to handle the maintenance** – Not you or your staff. Contract for maintenance. Make sure you go in and look once in a while to make sure your developer is actually staying on top of updates. Lots offer maintenance contracts and then only check quarterly, if at all.

  News of security vulnerabilities spread very quickly in the community. Hackers are part of the community. Maintenance on open source can't wait. If it were me, I would be doing updates immediately upon release.

- **Do not go with the cheapest developer** – There are reasons why they are the cheapest. Use only experienced developers, ones that know about the security, have used open source for years, and have done many open source sites. They will not be the cheapest. Make sure you get a written proposal for everything.

- **Before you buy, look at the websites your developer has done** – Don't just look, test them. Click the links. Fill out the forms. Try to break them. If you see a bunch of errors popping up, then keep looking for someone else.

- **Get a real designer** – If the developer is not a designer, make them work with a designer to get you a better looking website than any template can deliver. The image of your practice is important. Same applies to closed source.

- **Don't go too crazy with the plug-ins** – Find high quality plug-ins from developers who have been doing this a while. Not from someone doing it for the first time. Remember, the more plug-ins you have, the more maintenance you have to keep up with.

- **Stick with widely adopted open source software** – For a dental website, WordPress is probably the one that's more closely suited for the type and size of your business. If you are looking for lower cost, Wordpress is your best bet. Drupal or Joomla can also be used; however, they are larger CMS systems and they have a ton of features that you'll probably never use. Using Drupal or Joomla for a small website can be a little like using a Bazooka to kill a tweety-bird. You probably don't need all that power and complexity for a small website.

- **If you go Drupal, look into support contracts** – I can tell you the founder of Drupal himself realized that "community" support is pretty bad. So he set up a company—Acquia—to deliver paid support for Drupal. If you go Drupal, I recommend you check with Acquia about support. You don't have to use Acquia, but don't say

I didn't warn you. The free support from the "community" can be time consuming and frustrating.

About the Web Developers

To SOME PEOPLE, all web developers look the same. I want you to be more sophisticated than that. Since we are looking at building websites from a dental practice owner/manager perspective, I want to talk to you about the different types of developers and how the website developers approach building your website and the trade-offs of each approach.

When I explain the lay of the land with web developers, I like to use a similar industry that most people are familiar with—the home building industry. Maybe you've built a home. Even though these names may not be official website industry terms, I think you'll understand my analogy.

In home building, you have different types of homebuilders. From high-end to low-end you have custom homebuilders, production home-builders, and pre-fabricated homebuilders. Each type of homebuilder designs their product to meet the needs of the homeowner within the budget he or she has to work with.

On the high-end, we have the custom homebuilders. They build one home at a time, exactly as the buyer wants. The homes are usually larg-er; they have beautiful custom finishes inside, custom cabinets, home theaters, etc. The homes make a statement. Like the custom homebuild-ers, the custom web developers are the most skilled programmers.

In the middle price range are the production homebuilders. They build in much greater volume, pre-designed homes with a limited number of upgrades. By standardizing on some of the amenities and cutting out some of the bells and whistles, the production built home is more affordable than custom. Like production homebuilders, the skill level of production web developers is not as high as custom developers. Since they aren't building from the ground up, they don't need to be as skilled.

Finally, on the low-end of the price range are the prefabricated (pre-fab) homebuilders. They limit choices to the basics; they use factory technology such as robots to build homes that the low-end home buyer can afford. Some come as kits the home buyer can assemble himself to save money. Like the homebuilding industry, the skill level of the people in the factory creating the prefabricated homes is high. So are the skills of the people building the site builders. But it doesn't stop there. You have the people using the site builders to build the website. Typically that person is low or not skilled at all which will adversely affect the quality of the end product no matter how good the website builder is.

So, just like homebuilding, there is the price-quality trade-off. The type of web development company you engage (or the tool) you use will determine the quality of the website you get in the end. Choose wisely.

The Different Levels of Websites

SINCE YOU HAVE the lay of the land, I'll move through this next section rather quickly. The three levels of websites: custom websites, production websites, and prefabricated websites (do-it-yourself site builders). Let's talk about the specifics of each.

CUSTOM WEBSITES

Just like the homes, custom websites are at the high end. Even though prices have come down for custom websites over the past few years, it is still a bit more expensive to build a custom website because of the planning time spent upfront. Especially if you are requesting custom features that have never been created before.

The process to building a custom website involves you meeting with a custom developer, talking to them, giving them an understanding of what you want. The developer then comes up with a plan and builds it for you.

Advantages of Custom Websites:

- They are designed one at a time to the owner's specifications.
- They are the most flexible type of website.
- The website is totally unique to your practice.
- Anything is possible
- You get exactly what you want.

- Custom websites are far less likely to be copied. It has too much of your DNA in it. It is a lot more work for a thief.

Disadvantages of Custom Websites:

- The developer will have to ask more questions

- Estimates may be off due to custom work

- Higher finished cost

- It can take longer to build a custom site

How They Charge:

Custom developers typically charge either on a time and materials basis or an estimated fee for the project.

Advice for Custom Websites:

- **Let the developer handle everything including the hosting** – So there is no finger pointing.

- **Tell your developer everything that you know that you might want to have in the site both now and in the foreseeable future** – Why? So they can plan for it in the code. Programming code is a lot like concrete. Once it's set, it's hard to change. You want to make any changes in the planning stages, because once everything is already built you have to get the jackhammer out to make changes. If you tell the developer what you are thinking and they build it into the plan, even if it is for a future phase, it can be much less expensive when you are ready to go forward with Phase 2.

- **For the best site, clearly define the scope with a project plan** – Some people try to save money by scrimping on the planning phase. Bad idea. In most cases, proper planning will reduce cost significantly more than the little extra it costs.

- **Once you have the project plan, then get an estimate** – Make sure you budget 15% to 20% more than the estimate. If you change your mind a lot, double the estimate. Once the project starts, realize you can be part of the problem if you ask for changes or ask for more than is in your project plan.

- **If the developer has done similar jobs before, we recommend doing things on a time and materials basis rather than a fixed quote** – Developers don't want to over quote or under quote something. Over quote and they don't get the work. Under quote it and they either have an upset client or have work they have to eat. If you do the project plan and you have the clarity and you aren't making a bunch of changes, you should get the project done for less if the developer does it on a time and materials basis.

- **On cutting edge projects that have never been done by the developer before, ask for a fixed quote** – Even though most developers will build in sufficient fudge factors in their fixed fee estimates. The fudge factor is a guard against potential unforeseen issues and problems. There is always a chance the developer will underestimate a project if you are doing stuff that is state-of-the-art. If they hit a major snag, we have seen even the best developers go over 200-300%. However, most dental websites involve well established features and are not on the leading edge of technology. The 15% rule should be fine.

- **Go with a reputable company** – Check them out online or with the Better Business Bureau.

PRODUCTION WEBSITES

Production type websites, for our discussion, mean that the websites are starting with an established base code and certain features and functionality of your website are already built. That means some of the website functionality is locked in before you start. Your financial savings on the site comes as a result of the fact the developer doesn't have to do as much work to finish the website.

The sweet spot of open source software is building production websites. Not to say that you can't build a custom website using open source. You can. However, doing a totally custom website with open source software would defeat the main advantage of open source, which is using the free code base and plug-ins.

Advantages of production websites:

- It'll reduce your initial cost over custom-built sites
- You are not building from ground zero. You're starting at seventy-five to eighty percent done.
- If you are using open source, theoretically, someone else can take over.
- Your developer can add features to it either via plug-ins or custom coding.
- You can see rough layouts before buying.

Disadvantages of Production Websites:

- Since parts are standardized, they can be easily duplicated. There is potential for thieves copying your website.
- Some of the developers offer identical cookie-cutter websites, and with some of them, the only things that change are the name, address, bios, phone number and e-mail address of the practice.
- Developers can get lax on quality control.
- Lower prices in many cases dictate less service for the buyer.
- More plug-ins may mean more maintenance.
- Use of templates may mean potentially boring sites.

How They Charge:

Production developers can usually give you a fixed price for the website as long as you don't ask for anything out of the ordinary.

Advice on Production Websites:

- **If you get a production website, have it customized** – To me, an identical site is unacceptable. It is your image of your practice. You want to have a unique look. You want a look that reflects your personality. You definitely don't want to look exactly like another practice in town.

- **If you are buying a template, ask if anyone else is using this design** – Go check out their website. Using an identical template site is not a good idea.

- **Don't be the guinea pig** – Go with someone very familiar with the Content Management System you select. Make sure they have used the Content Management Platform before and have built a fair number of sites with it.

- **Get a company with a team to help you** – Nothing against the little guy, but there is just so much to know these days it is pretty much hopeless for one person to keep up with it all.

- **Go with a full-service developer** – You don't want just an assembler—somebody who just slaps these things together and doesn't give any support. The "love you and leave you" approach is fraught with peril.

- **Go with solid companies, let them host it** – With some, you don't have a choice. They host it as part of their Software As A Service (SAAS). And again, even with the production sites, ask if you can take it with you. Some of them you can, some you can't.

PREFABRICATED WEBSITES (SITE BUILDERS)

These are websites that are created using site builders, including pretty much all the domain registrars like GoDaddy.com or Network Solutions or the hosting companies like 1&1. Even Intuit offers a free site builder. Most are a waste of your time. Think about it; they can't give you anything too powerful or it would be a support nightmare for them. They are dealing in millions of domains. You will not be able to craft a quality image and achieve search engine rankings with these tools.

Advantages of Prefabricated Websites (Site Builders):

- They're cheap (usually free)
- Fast to set up
- Can make your own changes

Disadvantages of Prefabricated Websites (Site Builders):

- **You don't own it** – If you stop paying, it goes away.

- **These are general market tools** – So you will probably not find features specific to dentists.

- **You have to do all the heavy lifting** – In many cases, all you get is the website structure. You have to find and load all your own photos and write and place all your own copy.

- **Some site builders do not give you the ability to do Search Engine Optimization (SEO) on your website** – They just didn't build any way to add the code in the site builder. I guess they assume you're going to market some way other than doing anything online, which would be a huge mistake for a dental practice.

- **Support can be lacking**.

- **You may not be able to customize** – The ones you can't customize usually make it so you have to use templates.

- **Can't take it with you** – If you want out, it's a hassle to disengage. You're basically starting over so that you cannot take most of it with you.

- **Difficult or impossible to work with other outside technology**.

How They Charge:

Most are either free if you host with the company or you are charged a very low monthly amount. You stop paying your hosting or monthly bill and the whole website goes poof!

Advice for Prefabricated Websites (Site Builders):

- **My best advice is don't use them** – If you're going to ignore that advice and go this route, at least try several before you commit to one. Most of them have a trial period. If they don't deliver, I would walk away. No trial usually means it is worthless and they are trying to trap you. Do the trial; you will probably know in an hour if this tool is one you can work with.

- **Look for site builder reviews** – When considering a site builder, save time by Googling the "product name" review and see what other users have to say. If you see a large number of unhappy customers, pass on that builder.

- **Pass on ads** – One more thing...if it is ad driven or they're going to place advertising on your site, don't use it. Look for another one.

Reviewing the Proposals

OKAY. YOU HAVE done your research. Hopefully, I have been persuasive enough to kill off the thought of using a site builder. You know what type of site you are looking for. You have identified potential developers to work with. You have met with them. They have done their needs assessment on you. You have weighed all the factors. The developers have given you a written proposal. Just before you pull that trigger, there's one last thing I want you to double-check—the Site Map.

In the proposal there should be a document called a Site Map. The Site Map is a diagram of all the pages on your website along with the site navigation (flow) and the technology being used to drive your website. It is important to look closely at this document. Does it have all the pages? Does it have pages in the right order? Does it have contact forms? Is there anything missing?

The Site Map is the blueprint for your website. If you see something on the Site Map that you don't like or something you want to change, bring it up with the developer—**before** you sign. Most developer prices are based on your site map. You want it to be right so you know what you are getting. It is a whole lot easier to change a diagram on a piece of paper. Once they start building your website, it is much more difficult and costly to make changes.

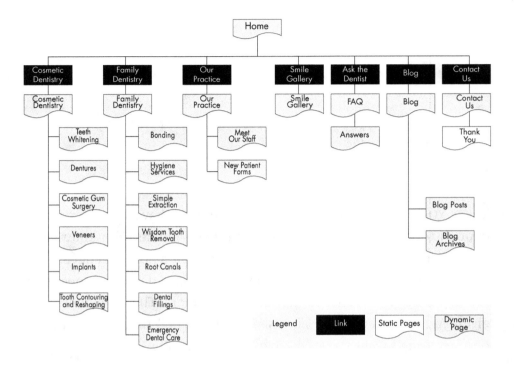

Does everything look good with the proposal and site map? Fantastic! Now it is time to pull the trigger.

THE WINNER IS . . .

You have made your decision. High five! You have accepted the proposal from one of the developers. The ink is dry on the agreement. The next two things you need to deal with are the domain and where the website will be hosted. Let's take them one at a time. First, the domain.

Securing and Managing Your Domain

YOUR DOMAIN NAME is also called a web address or URL. You've seen them as www. _____. com. This is what people type in their web browser to pull up your website. Usually, the first thing your web developer will ask you is a barrage of questions about the status of your domain. Do you have one? If so, who has control of it. If not, do you want one? If yes, what name? Unless you are technical, most people barely know where the information on their domain is, much less, who is the registrar.

SELECTING A DOMAIN NAME

You can get domains on your own, however, I strongly suggest asking your Internet Marketing company for help picking a domain name and then letting your web developer help you with obtaining your domain(s). Domain names have search engine implications. Even though this may be changing, it is best to get expert counsel on the selection of a domain name for your practice. Your domain name is important. Spend the time necessary to get the right one. You will be living with this decision for a long time.

Registrars

Registrars are the folks who you buy the domains from. The big name registrars are GoDaddy.com, Tucows.com, register.com, Network Solutions (netsol.com) and others. As the domain purchaser, you (or your company) are the registrant.

Domain Registration Periods

Domains are typically offered in one-year or two-year increments. FYI, you can buy them up to ten years at a time from a registrar. If I were you, I would do it for 10 years at a time. That way you don't have to mess with it as often and you have less chance of losing it. Though, once a year, you do need to make sure the info is still correct.

Controlling Your Domain

Once you have your domain, you don't want to lose it. If you're really, really, really good at managing your affairs, then you might want to register your own domain. You will still need to do some technical setup, so I don't usually recommend it. It really depends on the practice. I've seen some that were really good and on top of stuff and I've seen others who couldn't do it and lost their domain. If you have a solid website provider that is managing the domains, it's okay to let them handle renewals.

Renewals are one bill you do not want to miss. If you do miss a renewal, somebody else will likely buy that domain name and then ask you to pay them twenty times the cost of a renewal to get it back. If someone who wants to keep the domain and use it grabs it after expiration, you may never get it back. So don't miss the renewal payment.

Also, be aware, there are unscrupulous people out there who will try to trick you into switching your domain registration over to them. This is called domain slamming. They usually do this by sending official looking notices that say it is time for you to renew your domain. Make sure you know exactly who your domain is purchased through and when it is due. Don't be fooled by such domain slammer tricks.

Web Hosting

Once you have a domain, you need to have some place to host your website. Unless you have serious reasons for not doing so, I recommend you use your developer's recommended host. Better yet, let your developer handle everything. It helps avoid finger pointing. Developers usually have a favorite host. Going with their favorite can speed up development because they are familiar with the setup and tools. Before the developer gives you the name of a recommended host provider, I would let them know that you want a quality host and it doesn't have to be the rock bottom cheapest.

If you picked a developer that tells you they don't handle hosting and they want you to handle hosting on your own, you may seriously want to reconsider whether to use that developer. Hosting is too technical for most people. You don't want to get stuck doing your own hosting support. If they won't handle it, they are telling you they aren't that technical. Don't use them.

WHAT TO LOOK FOR IN YOUR WEB HOSTING COMPANY

Fast Website Load Time

One of the first things you want to check is the speed your website loads. Google closely watches how fast your website loads, and measures their own search engines in the number of milliseconds it takes to return your search results. Google has found that the slower search results come up, the less people search. It is hard to believe that a 250 milliseconds slower load time can make a difference in people's behavior. Google says it does. So they want your website to be lightning fast. I have been told, they actually factor in speed in their calculation of your rankings. So you want a website that loads fast.

Even if Google didn't matter, a slow loading website can affect your results. People do not wait around very long these days.

Quality E-mail Services

In 99% of the cases, your website host will also provide your email services. The 1% exception is if you host your own e-mail server. Only big companies with more than 100 email addresses to manage should even consider running their own e-mail server.

No matter who handles your e-mail server, e-mail is critical. You want to make sure that you get a host provider with solid e-mail services. By that I mean, too much downtime is unacceptable. Move to another hosting company if downtime is affecting your practice.

E-mail Addresses Matching Your Domain

Be sure to set up all your practice e-mail addresses to use your domain name. For example, if your name is Carol Parks and your practice name is Smile Dental Center and your domain is www.smiledentalcenter.com, set up your e-mail address using your domain name like carolparksdds@smiledentalcenter.com.

Do not use your personal e-mail address in your practice. Using personal e-mail addresses like carol4876@gmail.com or CP1444@AOL.com or DeathStar9@Yahoo.com for your practice email is just not professional.

The right way to do it is to get an e-mail address for everyone who needs one at the practice and to set up some role e-mail addresses too like accounting@YourDomainNameHere.com (for billing questions), appointments@YourDomainNameHere.com (to change/reschedule appointments), info@YourDomainNameHere.com (for inquires) and newsletter@YourDomainNameHere.com (if you plan to send out a newsletter). These are set up as alias e-mails meaning they will forward to someone else. The beauty is if someone leaves, you just forward the e-mail from the alias account to their replacement. Since the e-mail address hasn't changed, you don't have to send out notices that anything has changed.

If you have the right host, you give them a list of employee names and e-mail passwords and they will set up the accounts. Give them a list of role e-mails you want and the e-mail that they forward to. They will set them up for your practice.

Going to the trouble to integrate your domain name with your e-mail is well worth the effort. It is more professional, saves time and having your domain name on every e-mail going out is like a little mini advertisement for your practice.

No Canonicalization Issues

You want to make sure that your domain is set so no matter how people type it in—with or without the www.—it still goes to just one URL. If you don't fix this, people will technically be going to two different websites. Google will see it as two separate websites and split the traffic between the two websites.

Current on Website Security

Web hosting security is critical and you want to make sure that the web host knows what they're doing in applying security patches and has the ability to maintain your website. And you'll know if you constantly go down and somebody defaces your site that these are signs that security is an issue. If you are using open source make sure that you keep up with the updates.

VALUE VS. PRICE

Many people don't think a lot about web hosting. Lots of times, they just look for a low price. Basing your decision on price is certainly one way to do it, but perhaps it's not the wisest way. I believe it is far more important to have excellent service than to save a few dollars a month. Web hosting is actually very important to the success of your website.

What is the difference between high-level hosting and low-level hosting? Let's take two companies, one is going discount hosting at $10 a month and the other is going full-service hosting paying $50 a month. Both are giving service 24/7, every day. Ever stop and think about how much that is per hour? A month with 30 days has 720 hours. A $10 per month cost equals 1.3 cents per hour and a $50 per month cost equals 6.9 cents per hour—a difference of 5.6 cents per hour. Is it worth paying 5.6 cents more per hour? If everything were always fine then the answer would be "no." However, things aren't always fine.

Discount Hosting Providers

The discount hosts are usually managing an extremely large number of websites. Some literally can be managing millions of websites. Most of these are set up for open source hosting. Yes, they use free open source software to run the servers too.

As you might imagine, if you need support and your host manages many millions of domains it can be hard to get their attention. You may be paying $2 a month. One phone call can wipe out their profit for several years. So what do they do? At some hosting companies you can't talk with a human. They put up a c-panel (control panel) and that's it. If you're lucky enough to have a support number to call, don't mistakenly believe that they will actually help you with anything. They expect you to manage your domains, website and e-mail yourself through the control panel. The only help you are able to get is if you don't have permission to set up something you need. They will also help if you need to change service levels, need help restoring from backup or help if your website is down. Trust me, they probably won't notice if your site is down. They have far too many websites to worry about. You have to call them and let them know it is down. Here is how the call typically goes with a discount host . . .

If you call, you get a front line screener person who really can't help you. The front line screener can generally answer a few basic questions. In my experience, about all they can do is entertain you and then forward your request to a second layer technical support person. The second layer can do a few more things than the front line. If there is real trouble, you might get passed to a third layer. The third layer is generally an over-worked senior engineer. Usually, this is where your problem is really solved. Believe me, it can be frustrating to claw your way through the layers if you have a real problem. We have experienced several hosting companies where it took days to go through all three layers.

If you go with a large host, you probably want to sign up for a monitoring service. They have so many websites it is very hard to effectively monitor them all. If they have a big problem and many sites go down they will catch it; however, if just your site has a problem they probably won't see that it is down.

I am sorry if I have offended any discount hosts. I am sure there are exceptions. Unfortunately, this has been our experience over many years with several different discount hosting providers. We understand the economics at $2 a month hosting. We just don't understand why they (and their customers) want to live like that.

Full-Service Host Providers

There are many types of hosting companies out there. I can't speak about specific offerings by any of them except our own company. To give you contrast, here is what you may expect if you are on our $50 per month plan (comes out to around 6.9 cents per hour) . . .

We provide a server to house your web site and its log files (in many cases can be over one Gb in size). Our servers run Microsoft server software and Microsoft SQL databases. We provide all the software licenses for these servers. We provide backups of the website. We have two connections to the Internet, one to handle your data and one as a backup connection in case the first connection fails. We provide e-mail servers and software to handle your e-mail. There are so many people sending spam these days that we have hardware and software designed to knock out 95% of spam before it gets to your in box. We provide intrusion detection hardware and software for security. We have systems for monitoring server room temperatures. We have systems for monitoring server up time. These will notify us if something fails. We have an Inergen gas fire suppression system, so if a fire breaks out in the server room we don't have to use water to put it out. Water has a nasty way of ruining electronic devices. We have two a/c systems. One to cool and the other just in case the first one fails. Even though we are on the same electrical power grid as a hospital, we have a back up generator that can run for several weeks in case the power company can't deliver power. We offer trained IT people to watch over all of this, we provide phone support by the actual IT people who watch over the systems. We also provide management of your website domains so you don't miss a renewal.

To wrap up the discount vs. full-service hosting discussion, at least to me, there is a strong correlation to the amount you pay and the service you get. If you don't mind fixing things yourself when they break or mind working your way through layers of people to resolve issues to save $480 a year, then consider discount hosting. To me, my time is worth more than that.

Say "No" To Hosting Your Own Website

If you have someone who suggests you host your website on your own in-house servers, just say "no" to that idea. Do not try to do hosting yourself. The cost to do it yourself is very high and your needs are probably very modest. A professional hosting company can easily handle your needs. That way, you don't have to buy all the equipment and licenses yourself. Servers and licenses are many thousands of dollars a year. Don't listen to the cable guy trying to talk you into it. He doesn't have to buy all the equipment.

These are just some of the considerations of hosting. If you find a good company to work with, you won't have to mess with any of these technical details yourself.

Web Design

WEB DESIGN ENCOMPASSES many different areas. Some areas are more subjective, like the look and feel of the website, while other areas are more objective including the structure and site navigation. For our discussion, we'll be talking about the front-end of a website (what the user sees). Before we get into the parts of design, let's answer one important question . . .

WHY IS WEB DESIGN IMPORTANT?

In a lot of cases, the website is the first place that somebody will go to check up on you. It is the first impression of your practice. As we know, you don't get a second chance at a first impression. If your website is done right, it will make people perceive your practice as the high quality practice that you are. They will know they want to schedule an initial visit with you. Done incorrectly, it can leave people with a negative impression of your practice. In just a few seconds on your website, these prospective patients can make up their mind then and there whether or not you are the dentist for them.

Time Required for a Great Design

Design is like polishing an apple. The longer you polish it, the nicer it will look. Ask the designer how many hours they are planning to spend on design. We have found that it takes a minimum of 25 hours or more to produce a high quality design. If you have a large site with complex navigation it can take longer than that. You want to give them enough time to really polish that apple. It also helps to find a highly skilled designer.

About half the searches nowadays are from mobile devices. You want to make sure you either do a separate mobile site or the latest solution is to create your website with a responsive design. That is a design that adapts to the display size of the device that is accessing it. That can take longer to design but it does prevent you from having to build and manage multiple websites.

SITE STRUCTURE

Site structure (the way the website is built) and site navigation (flow of the site) can dramatically affect traffic and lead conversion. What you want is a website that allows visitors to know where they are on the site and how to find what they're looking for quickly and easily.

All sites have an underlying flow. If it's haphazard, visitors and the search engine can get confused. If visitors are confused, they leave. If the search engines get confused, it will affect your search engine rankings.

So when discussing web design, just know it is more than the look and feel of the website. It also includes the navigation and the structure of the site.

DESIGN CHOICES: CUSTOM DESIGN OR TEMPLATE

The main choices for creating your web design are getting a designer to create a custom design (totally unique to you), or going out and finding an acceptable design, templates or theme (in many cases templates may be used or resold to others).

The Process for a Custom Design

The designer will talk with you to get an impression of your practice.

They get a feel for the image you want to portray. They go away and build a design mock up. The design mock up is an easily edited visual representation of your page(s). It looks just like a web page only it doesn't have any functionality like clickable buttons, mouse rollovers or changing images. It is very easy to make changes in the mock up phase. Once you are happy with the design, the designer will convert it into a working website complete with functionality.

The Process When Using Design Templates

The person building your site goes out and finds a template design as the basis of your website. They show it to you. If you like it, they will buy it. If not, they will keep looking. Templates are generally very cheap, usually under $100. The site builder gets the template and changes out some of the content and then integrates it into the software they are using to run the website.

Notice, on the template process I said "the person building your website." I didn't say "designer". The template builder in many cases is not a designer. Programmers love templates because most of them can't design. My theory on it is to be a great programmer they predominately use the logical left side of the brain. Designers predominately use the creative right side of the brain. When it comes to the look of your site, get the right brain folks working for you.

ADVICE ON WEB DESIGN:

- **Get a good eye** – Beauty is in the eye of the beholder. If you want a great looking site, make sure the one approving your website design has an "eye" for design. Where does the "eye" for design come from? I don't know. I think it may be genetic. All I know is some people have it and some don't. But I do know that it is real. I've seen it. You've seen it. Just look closely at any Apple product. The folks designing their products have an "eye" for design. Every detail, even the packaging is art.

To cut to it, if you do not have an art or design or advertising or marketing background then chances are you don't have a trained "eye" for design. Don't be offended. There are always exceptions. There is no shame if you need help in this area. If you have trouble color coordinating your own outfits, that's a sign. If you know you don't have an "eye" for design, it's best to hire an expert designer or get an expert opinion on the design of your website. My personal advice is even if you do have an "eye" for design, always use someone with design skills to come up with your website design.

• **Go with a custom design** – Unless you are just short on cash, go with a custom design. It is easier on you and you will most likely wind up with a much superior end product. Life is too short to own an ugly website. I like to have it my way. Custom gives you beauty and things the way you want it. After all, you are probably only going to do a website every few years. You want it to be a good one if it is going to represent you. Most times, we are only talking a couple thousand dollars difference. The difference in appearance is huge.

The dental industry has it extra tough. The regulations on dental marketing restrict you from saying too much and many consumers believe that all dentists are the same. It is hard to stand out. If you are going to start breaking down those perceptions of sameness, you need to start with the first impression of your practice. The first impression is most likely going to be set by your website. If you want to stand out, go with a custom design that reveals a bit of your personality. It's worth it to make sure no other practice will look just like yours.

• **Show your personality and consistency in your website design** – This is easy if you go with a custom design. You just tell the designer. If you are not going custom, then you'll need to find a template that is the closest fit. When you're looking through templates there are many different kinds—some are high-tech looking, some are more friendly, some are old, some are modern, some are country, some are for kids. There are thousands. You want to find the one that kind of matches your personality in your practice.

- **Be consistent** – The bottom line is that you want to make sure there are no major differences between your image on your website and your real life practice. That means when clients come to your practice after visiting your website, it feels like a continuation of what they saw online. Do it right and the new patient feels comfortable. Do it wrong and the new patient will feel misled. To appreciate this point, have you ever had this experience? You've booked a hotel online. In the pictures, the hotel looks like a palace. You get there and it looks more like a shack. Don't you feel misled?

  So, make sure the website design is consistent with your practice. Don't have someone do an ultra modern, high-tech looking website if your practice is sporting furniture from the 70's. If you do, there's likely to be a disconnect when the patient arrives at your office. That shiny new patient off the Internet may bail on you once they see your real office.

- **Tie in your logo and match the colors** – Logos can add a lot to the polish of your website. Incorporating your logo color into your design can be a very nice look. If you don't have a logo, they're not hard to get. Your development company can help you get one, but if you want a good consistent look, it has to represent part of your identity. And just because you did this logo a long time ago doesn't mean you have to stick with it. You can have a graphic designer refresh your logo or even do a new one.

  Before you say "no" to a new logo, at least check out the cost. I've been in marketing a long time. Back in the day, logos were scary expensive. But now it's not like that. There are many more people doing it. The tools are available and you've got designers all over the world willing to take a shot at it. So there are many options now. I mean you can get logos for a couple hundred bucks.

- **Do not go cheap on design** – For a quarter more you can go first-class. Find a highly skilled designer and give them time to create something great.

- **Get a real designer involved** – Even if you decide to go with a template, get a designer to customize it for you. Make sure they do a site plan. That way, they will know all the elements the website needs to include. If you get someone who is not a designer, I don't care how great a template they get, it will be an inferior product to one created by a real designer. A true designer will see things that will enhance your design that a "non-designer" would never think of. I have seen designers use part of a photo and then alter it in Photoshop to give an amazing visual effect. Basically, all a non-designer might be able to do is square photos on a solid background.

- **Make sure your design is mobile compatible** – Do a separate mobile site or build your website with a responsive design.

Finally, here are some of the things you want to make sure your web design accomplishes . . .

- The visitors feel the quality of your practice.

- The visitors are impressed with your ability to give them high quality treatment.

- The visitors get a sense of who you are.

- The visitors are informed about what you can do for them.

- The visitors understand why your practice is special.

- Important parts of the website are clearly highlighted.

- Visitors are able to easily navigate the website.

- The visitors find what they are looking for—directions, phone numbers, etc.

- The website motivates visitors to make an appointment.

- Visitors are directed to the action or actions you want them to take.

Website Add-On Features

THERE ARE A few more features that you might want to consider adding to your website. These may or may not be part of the core offering of your website. If they aren't, don't worry. They can be added to your website later. But make sure the Site Plan allows for them.

ONLINE APPOINTMENT SETTING

Online appointment setting allows the patient to go to the website or use their mobile device to book and change appointments on their own. This feature is one you really want to look at, depending on the technical sophistication of your users. If your patients are primarily a young, tech-savvy bunch, you might want to consider this. Young, tech-savvy, time-pressed people can be heavy mobile users and want to do everything using a mobile phone or tablet.

If most of your patients are seniors, this is probably not a real high priority. The reasoning is that most seniors are "old school" and prefer to deal with a person. This could change going forward.

Like anything, there are pros and cons. The pros are online appointment setting is convenient for the patient and it saves staff time. The cons are your appointment data can wind up in two places and online appointment setting can make it too easy to cancel or change appointments at the last minute. It is probably better to have your patients talk to someone in order to get out of their appointment.

WEB VIDEO

Video is important for several reasons . . .

- Video gives visitors a look at you and your practice.
- Video can help improve your search engine rankings.
- Video makes your website more interesting.
- Video makes your website more engaging.
- You can communicate things in video that you can't in any other way.

We strongly recommend you take a look at adding video to your website.

If you do decide to incorporate video, be sure to hire a professional videographer. Just like with websites, with all the new tools making it easier to create, there are many amateur video producers out there. Trust me, some things are better left to the professionals.

We tried doing our own video in-house. We weren't terrible at it. However, since then, we've brought on several professional video people to work with us. Now having seen the difference between a do-it-yourself project and a professionally produced product, there is no comparison. Hands down, the video done by the professionals is superior.

I know YouTube has spawned a whole generation of wannabe stars who have recorded their personal antics on a video camera. That's fine if you're just fooling around with your friends. In this case, you are not fooling around. At least I hope not! You are a professional service provider. You need a professional business image and amateur video is not the way to get there.

PRACTICE REVIEW SOFTWARE

If you would like to have reviews on your website, there are many ways of going about this. You can have a developer create a review section on your website or there are software companies offering add-on products to handle and automate these for you.

Having patients give reviews can be a two-edged sword. They help build your credibility if the reviews are positive. They hurt credibility if a high number of the reviews are negative. Unless you build review software into your website, you're probably not going to have total control over what is posted.

If you decide to have an outside company to handle the review portion, beware of a few things...

Some services won't let you take any comments off - If you see that the service you are considering including on your website allows anonymous comments, I would pass. There is nothing like a nasty negative comment and you don't know who posted it. You can't even find out so you can call and try to get it straightened out.

Some services let you take stuff off but are a real pain to deal with - They want to investigate. Is it a legit comment? We don't want to stifle the community by censoring. Meanwhile, the comment could be seriously affecting your practice.

Advice on Practice Review Software:

- **Look for negative comments** – Sign up for Google Alerts to monitor for anything going up with your name on it. It isn't perfect, however, we have caught some things early with it.

- **Don't freak out if you get a bad review now and then** – It happens. It is normal. I used to own a marketing research company. Just like comment cards and voluntary surveys, you get the extreme on both ends. Either you get the real happy people or the real unhappy people. You generally don't get the folks in the middle. The reason? The folks in the middle don't feel strongly enough to give you their opinion. If you get a bad review, call the patient immediately and try to get the issue resolved.

- **Reviews are optional, think before you add them** – You need to decide whether or not you think that the reviews would be primarily positive. How many complaints do you normally get? Do you have any really unhappy patients? All it takes is one very unhappy patient with lots of free time. I have seen them on a mission to make life very difficult for the person they are obsessed with. If that is you, it can really hurt your practice.

- **Either build your own reviews into your site or look for companies offering more control over reviews** – Look for services where, for the most part, you can control what goes up on your site.

- **If you are very confident, use the services with reviews open to the world** – I have been told they carry more weight in the search engines.

We are now going to move from possible add-on features to a little bit about the content of your website.

Building Traffic to Your Website

U̶P UNTIL NOW we have been talking about how to build a great website for your practice. Now we need to talk about how you go about getting visitor traffic to that website.

There is no law that says all website marketing must be done online. If you're doing any offline marketing, such as ads in publications, card decks, newsletters, mailing post cards, flyers, sponsoring events, handing out appointment cards, business cards or reprinting your letterhead, make sure you are promoting your web address on every single piece of your written materials.

If you are still in the yellow pages, make sure your web address is on there. If you have a great website, it will boost the effectiveness of all your offline forms of advertising.

You can promote your practice via traditional offline methods; however, you will most likely find that you can get a lot more folks to your website if you promote it online. Plus, there is a built-in advantage to doing online marketing—the people are already using their computer or mobile device.

The real mission of your marketing is to let people know your practice is an option for dental care in their area.

INTERNET MARKETING

Internet Marketing is the big umbrella term for all the types of things you do to build qualified visitor traffic to your website using online methods.

Why Is It Important?

Internet Marketing seeks to bring visitors to your website and convert them to leads or sales. You may have heard the expression, "If you don't build website traffic, your website is like a billboard in the desert." It is true. The only leads you get from your website will be from your visitor traffic. If you have the right traffic (potential patients from your area) and the right content (including the right message) the chances that they will contact you goes up.

Do-It-Yourself vs. Outsourcing

There are many options for marketing your web site online. More come out practically every day. We will go over the majors here. If you want to know more, you can. Believe me, there are many books written on each one of these topics individually. My advice is to hire someone to market your website for you. You can either spend a very significant amount of time learning about Internet marketing to use it a handful of times in your life, or you can simply hire someone who already knows it and studies it and let them do it.

Search Engine Marketing

You definitely want to be found in the search engines. Search engines like Google, Bing and Yahoo are where people go to find information. The visitor traffic coming from search engines provides some of the richest sources of new patient leads the Internet has to offer.

There are several ways to be found in the search engines. Let's talk about each of them.

Organic Search Marketing - Search Engine Optimization (SEO)

There's organic search marketing. We like organic results the best because once you have your website indexed, meaning it appears in the search engine, all the traffic coming from the organic search listings is free traffic.

Here is what it typically requires to get good ranking. Money. It is very technical work and you really need a skilled Internet Marketer versed in search engine optimization techniques to rank high in the search engines.

The Internet search engines are always changing. For example, Google alone does about 500 changes a year on their search engine. Keeping up with that much change can be very time consuming.

As a dental practice, you don't need anywhere near a full-time person to optimize your website for the search engines. Part-time will do fine. However, you do want someone who's skilled, experienced and familiar with best practices. No doubt you want to have SEO done on your website.

Paid Search Marketing - Search Engine Marketing (SEM)

Paid Search Marketing goes by several names... Search Engine Marketing (SEM) or Pay Per Click (PPC) advertising. Paid Search Marketing has to do with creating, managing and placing the little advertisements that show up around organic search results. The listings generally show up above and to the right of the organic results. See the boxes in the example results page below.

One way to use PPC ads is if you're just getting started marketing your website and you have no traffic going to your website because your website is not ranked organically in the search engines. To get traffic quickly, it's a good idea to buy PPC ads. The reason? It takes some time for the organic search rankings to show up. With PPC ads you can have traffic immediately. Then as your other Internet Marketing kicks in, you can weigh and decide whether or not to continue the PPC advertising.

Local Search

When we first started in the search marketing business in the 1990's, if you got ranking in the search engines and directories, it was for the whole country (in some cases, the whole world). The search engines didn't stay that way for long. They realized it was way too broad to be useful for most searches. They saw a large amount of searches included geographic qualifiers. So, they now identify where the searcher is and display results for a smaller geographic area called Local Search. Now Local Search is a huge part of the search engine's searches.

Not only can search engines like Google tell where the person is and what they are searching for, Google is also learning about the person's search habits and is trying to customize the search experience for the individual.

I think it is probably rare that people fly in from other states to get to your office. You are most likely drawing from a local area right around your practice. If this is true, you want to focus most of your marketing efforts on local search. You want a strong presence in your local area. Be sure to tell your Internet Marketing Company what geographical area you pull from. Then have them focus their efforts to make sure you come up for searches for dentists in this area. Local search—this is something that all dentists should be focused on.

Organic Search Marketing, Paid Search Marketing and Local Search are the main parts of Search Engine Marketing. There are still other types of Internet Marketing for you to consider.

BLOGGING

Blogging (short for web logging) is writing articles on topics relevant to dentistry and posting them on your website or a blog site. These blogs can really help boost your rankings in the search engines. The bad news is they take a lot of time to do. I recommend you let someone else write blogs for you and then you review them before they are posted. Even though they are valuable to the search engines, your time is too valuable to spend blogging.

DIRECTORIES

Directories are websites that list various types of businesses. Some are free and some are paid listings. There are only a handful of directories worth paying to be in.

Examples of good ones are Yahoo.com, Angie's List and the Better Business Bureau. Make sure to have any directory you are considering evaluated by your Internet Marketing Company as to whether they're good bets or not for your practice.

Google has put heavy penalties on some directory websites for paid listings. Some were penalized so badly, it will actually hurt your website rankings to be in them.

EMAIL MARKETING AND NEWSLETTERS

Sending email and newsletters to patients can be a great way to stay in touch. You do want to be respectful of people and ask their permission to send to them. If you want to send out e-mail newsletters, it is best to do that through an e-mail marketing company.

Two companies we have found to be very reputable are Mail Chimp at http://www.mailchimp.com, and Constant Contact at http://www.constantcontact.com.

SOCIAL MEDIA MARKETING

As soon as we got connected with each other, we started to form on-line communities. These communities evolved into what is now called social media—MySpace in 2003, Facebook in 2004, YouTube in 2005 and Twitter in 2006. No doubt social networks are another global game changer that is underway. Social networks have already changed the world. You have seen the fall of dictatorships because of them.

Social Media can be fertile ground for marketing opportunities for your business. The trouble is that marketing using social media is complex. Many business people are still scratching their head on how to use it to market their business. Fear not, like any radical change it takes a while to figure things out. Already, there are target marketing opportunities like we've only dreamed about. My advice? Get some help and get involved now. Your survival may depend on it.

Social Media Marketing is a little outside the scope of this book. But at least let me get you a lay of the land. The four main players now are Facebook, LinkedIn, Twitter and Google+.

Facebook is by far the largest social network. There are roughly seven billion people on the planet. Facebook has over a billion users worldwide. Yes. You can reach one out of seven in the world using Facebook.

In the U.S., over 50% of the population is on Facebook. That's one out of every two people. Facebook can be locally focused and is for communicating with your friends (and in many cases friends of your friends). Local friends of friends are where your practice growth may come from.

Right now, Facebook is designed more for people to connect with other people. Socializing businesses on Facebook still feels a little awkward. Facebook is trying to change that. The jury is still out on whether people will embrace businesses like people. My advice is to test using Facebook ads to target potential patients in your area. Send the traffic to your website instead of directly to your business Facebook page.

Another social network you may have heard about is LinkedIn. *LinkedIn* is more for people seeking employment and recruiters. It is a social network that has some good groups that you could participate in; however, this is not where you'll probably find many patients. I would pass on investing a lot of time in LinkedIn unless you need to recruit staff.

Twitter is not really geography focused. It literally covers the whole world. While you can look for people in the local area it isn't ideal. For this reason I can't recommend it as a great way to promote your dental practice. Mess with Twitter after you become famous.

Google+ is Google's third or fourth attempt at a social network. It is well done. However, it is for more technical people. It doesn't have a fraction of Facebook's user base. I recommend you get signed up with Google+ for what it will do for your practice in the Google search engine. Other than that, I recommend you invest social media time in Facebook.

INTERNET MARKETING ADVICE:

- **Get a really good web presence first** – You know that will help your practice. Then start getting up to speed with the other things like social media. It's about priorities. Do small bites. Creep, crawl, walk, run to get up to speed.

- **Setup Google Analytics** – Make sure that Google Analytics is set up on your website to measure the results you are getting. If not Google Analytics, then set up some other analytics software. Without analytics, you are flying blind.

- **Focus on local search first** – Focus on your local search first because that's where most of your patients are going to find you.

- **Get help getting setup with Google+ Local** – It looks easy. However, if you don't do it right, it can be a nightmare to get corrected. Get some help with that.

- **Just say "no" to link building** – For years, one of the major strategies for increasing organic search rankings was link building. The reason was that the major factor in Google's PageRank algorithm was the number and quality of websites linking to your website. These links to your website are called "backlinks". The way Google sees it, if other websites consider you an authority and link to your website, your website must be important. Being important can seriously raise your rankings.

People figured out that if you could get a bunch of people to give you backlinks your ranking would go up. A whole new industry was born. It worked for years. That has all changed.

Google has declared war on low value websites created for the sole purpose of backlinking to other websites. Google came out with a special on-going update to identify these backlink sites and penalize any websites that are linked to them. It worked.

Much of this backlinking work was coming out of India. We have read cases recently saying U.S. companies with too many backlinks from India are being penalized in some search engines.

Be warned. Google will nuke your organic search rankings if you do any of the following: 1) Pay to get links; 2) Get a bunch of low value spammy backlinks; 3) Get a bunch of links faster than normal; and 4) Have an unnatural number of websites linking to you. The "good old" days of backlinking are over. So the advice is don't do link building. Build traffic by providing solid content people want to see.

- **Use PPC Marketing in the beginning to build traffic fast** – PPC is the fastest way to get results. It is a great way to test ads and ad copy quickly. You can directly target the keywords and have precisely worded ads.

- **Focus on building strong content** – Google wants you to have strong content. Have your website content evaluated. Make sure you have no duplicate content. If you can't write well, have someone else handle this for you.

- **Get involved with social media now** – You really should start getting involved with social media like Facebook immediately. I've been reading the marketing tea leaves for years. Social media has huge momentum. We are starting to see how social media can be harnessed for marketing purposes. Playing catch up is very hard. You want to get involved now in the earlier stages.

- **Don't go crazy time-wise on social media** – Social media can suck a bunch of your time. If you can, let others do it for you.

Conclusion

THE INTERNET HAS fundamentally changed buyer behavior, the way people look at the world, the way they find information and the way they buy. Just consider how you look for information and resources. I'm sure you go to the Internet, just like your patients and prospective patients.

So move over newspapers, magazines and yellow pages. New digital forms of media are taking over while the old forms of media are declining fast.

So it is—the world is changing. Where it is all going? No one knows for sure. About all I can guarantee is it will never be the same.

People are using the Internet to search for information. If your practice is reliant on traditional media to get new patients, you need to change now, because what you are relying on today is going to stop working. Not only has the media changed, the skills needed to market your practice have changed too. In addition to marketing knowledge, it takes technical expertise to be successful in today's online marketing world.

You need to ask a very tough question. I don't know who you might be using to market your practice these days. If you're using the same marketing person who helped you over the past twenty-plus years, you need to ask yourself this question—are they really keeping up with all the changes? If they are not, as hard as it may be, you really might want to consider changing to another marketing person or company.

I am not picking on older marketing folks. I am one of them. I am just pointing out that your marketing people must be up on the technology, the media, and the Internet. That's because when it comes to looking for a dentist, search engines and the web are where the people are looking. If you aren't represented there, you'll find it harder and harder to get new patients. Someone who doesn't know the Internet can't help you with online marketing.

Looking back at my 22 years in the business, the Internet has changed everything. I can't think of a single business or industry that hasn't been impacted by it. Change is scary. It has a nasty way of uprooting things we've come to depend on. In a just a few short years, dental marketing completely changed. Going forward, new technologies and new ways of connecting will continue to shape our future.

The good news...some things never change.

People will continue to need dental care. However, how these potential new patients go out and find a dental professional to serve them has changed.

People will continue to ask for referrals. However, they won't stop there. Most people, even when referred, will check out your website before they make the initial appointment. You owe it to yourself and the people who work for you to get your website right. It may be a slight over-simplification but, a good website equals a good company, and a bad website equals a bad company. Your website creates the first impression of your practice. Make sure it is a great one. Best wishes for success.

Dave

About The Author

David J. Larson is the founder and President of Sales & Marketing Technologies, a leading full-service web development and Internet marketing company.

Before founding Sales & Marketing Technologies, Dave co-founded New Directions Marketing Research, a full-service marketing research company. Utilizing focus group and survey research, the company provided primary research information to corporations and organizations operating in Florida. Some of the clients included: Orange County, Orlando Regional Medical Center, National Research Group, Disney and Universal Studios.

Prior to New Directions Marketing Research, Dave was involved in the computer industry. His knowledge of computers led to employment with the following companies: Entre' Computer Centers, Coordinated Financial Services, Connecticut General Insurance and Rax Restaurants of Florida.

Dave has served as President of the Orlando Chapter of the American Marketing Association and on the Board of the Orlando Advertising Federation. He has also served as a member of the Advertising Review Board of the Better Business Bureau. Dave was a member of the Czech-Mate project, an AMA sponsored marketing mission to Czechoslovakia. He is past President of Phi Theta Kappa national honor fraternity and recipient of the Florida Blue Key Award for Leadership.

You can connect with Dave online in any of the following ways:

Facebook: www.facebook.com/davidjlarson

Twitter: twitter.com/davidjlarson

Email: dlarson@smtdentalmarketing.com

Book Website: http://DentalWebsitesDemystified.com

Company Website: http://SMTDentalMarketing.com

About Sales & Marketing Technologies

Sales & Marketing Technologies (SMT) is a full-service web development and Internet marketing company headquartered in Altamonte Springs, Florida. Founded in 1991, SMT creates, develops and markets web sites for the healthcare industry.

Sales & Marketing Technologies can help with any of the services discussed in this book. To find out more, please visit Sales & Marketing Technologies' dental website at http://SMTDentalMarketing.com

If you are interested in speaking with Sales & Marketing Technologies about the needs of your practice, the fastest way is to call 407-682-2222 or Toll-Free 1-800-434-0339 or fill out the contact form on http://SMTDentalMarketing.com.